How to Analyze the Films of

TIM
BURTON

by Sun Hee Teresa Lee

ABDO
Publishing Company

Essential Critiques

How to Analyze the Films of

TIM BURTON

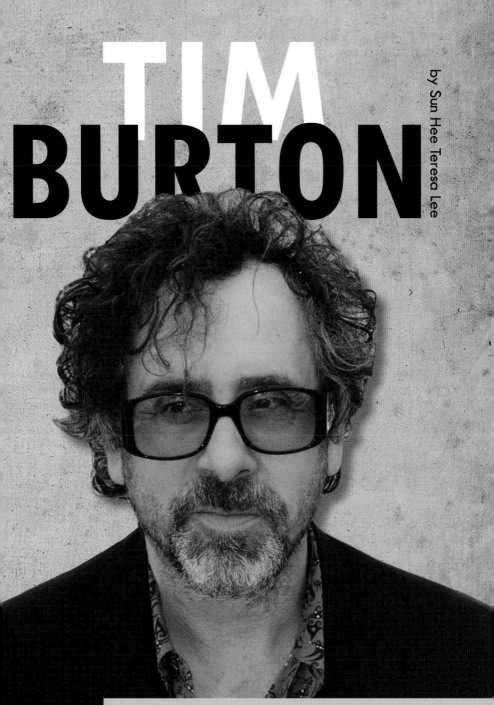

by Sun Hee Teresa Lee

Content Consultant: Michele Schreiber, PhD
assistant professor, Department of Film Studies, Emory University

Credits

Published by ABDO Publishing Company, 8000 West 78th Street, Edina, Minnesota 55439. Copyright © 2012 by Abdo Consulting Group, Inc. International copyrights reserved in all countries. No part of this book may be reproduced in any form without written permission from the publisher. The Essential Library™ is a trademark and logo of ABDO Publishing Company.

Printed in the United States of America,
North Mankato, Minnesota
062011
092011

Editor: Mari Kesselring
Copy Editor: Sarah Beckman
Interior Design and Production: Christa Schneider
Cover Design: Marie Tupy

Library of Congress Cataloging-in-Publication Data
Lee, Sun Hee Teresa.
  How to analyze the films of Tim Burton / by Sun Hee Teresa Lee.
      p. cm. -- (Essential critiques)
  Includes bibliographical references and index.
  ISBN 978-1-61783-089-1
  1. Burton, Tim, 1958---Criticism and interpretation--Juvenile literature. 2. Film
criticism--Juvenile literature. I. Title.
  PN1998.3.B875L44 2011
  791.4302'33092--dc22
                                        2011007389

Table of Contents

1

Introduction to Critiques

What Is Critical Theory?

What do you usually do as a member of an audience watching a movie? You probably enjoy the settings, the costumes, and the sound track. You learn about the characters as they are developed through dialogue and other interactions. You might be drawn in by the plot of the movie, eager to find out what happens next. Yet these are only a few of many ways of understanding and appreciating a movie. What if you are interested in delving more deeply? You might want to learn more about the director and how his or her personal background is reflected in the film. Or you might want to examine what the film says about society—how it depicts the roles of women and minorities, for example. If so, you have entered the realm of critical theory.

Critical theory helps you learn how various works of art, literature, music, theater, film, and other endeavors either support or challenge the way society behaves. Critical theory is the evaluation and interpretation of a work using different philosophies, or schools of thought. Critical theory can be used to understand all types of cultural productions.

There are many different critical theories. If you are analyzing a movie, each theory asks you to look at the work from a different perspective. Some theories address social issues, while others focus on the director's life, what role the direction plays in the overall film, or the time period in which the film was written or set. For example, the critical theory

that asks how a director's life affected the work is
called biographical criticism. Other common, broad
schools of criticism include historical criticism,
feminist criticism, auteur criticism, and ideological
criticism.

What Is the Purpose of Critical Theory?

Critical theory can open your mind to new ways
of thinking. It can help you evaluate a movie from
a new perspective, directing your attention to issues
and messages you may not otherwise recognize in
a work. For example, applying feminist criticism to
a film may make you aware of female stereotypes
perpetuated in the work. Applying a critical theory
to a work helps you learn about the person who
created it or the society that enjoyed it. You can
explore how the movie is perceived by current
cultures.

How Do You Apply Critical Theory?

You conduct a critique when you use a critical
theory to examine and question a work. The theory
you choose is a lens through which you can view
the work, or a springboard for asking questions
about the work. Applying a critical theory helps you

to think critically about the work. You are free to question the work and make an assertion about it. If you choose to examine a film using biographical criticism, for example, you want to know how the director's personal background inspired or shaped the work. You could explore why the director was drawn to the story. For instance, are there any parallels between a particular character's life and the director's life?

Forming a Thesis

Ask your question and find answers in the work or other related materials. Then you can create a thesis. The thesis is the key point in your critique. It is your argument about the work based on the tenets, or beliefs, of the theory you are using. For example, if you are using biographical criticism to ask how the director's life inspired the work, your thesis could be worded as follows: Director Teng Xiong, raised in refugee camps in Southeast Asia, drew upon her experiences to direct the movie *No Home for Me*.

> ### How to Make a Thesis Statement
>
> In a critique, a thesis statement typically appears at the end of the introductory paragraph. It is usually only one sentence long and states the author's main idea.

Providing Evidence

Once you have formed a thesis, you must provide evidence to support it. Evidence might take the form of examples and quotations from the work itself—such as dialogue from a film. Articles about the movie or personal interviews with the director might also support your ideas. You may wish to address what other critics have written about the work. Quotes from these individuals may help support your claim. If you find any quotes or examples that contradict your thesis, you will need to create an argument against them. For instance: Many critics have pointed to the heroine of *No Home for Me* as a powerless victim of circumstances. However, through her dialogue and strong actions, she is clearly depicted as someone who seeks to shape her own future.

How to Support
a Thesis Statement

A critique should include several arguments. Arguments support a thesis claim. An argument is one or two sentences long and is supported by evidence from the work being discussed.

Organize the arguments into paragraphs. These paragraphs make up the body of the critique.

In This Book

In this book, you will read overviews of famous movies by director Tim Burton, each followed by a critique. Each critique will use one theory and apply it to one work. Critical thinking sections will give you a chance to consider other theses and questions about the work. Did you agree with the author's application of the theory? What other questions are raised by the thesis and its arguments? You can also find out what other critics think about each particular film. Then, in the You Critique It section in the final pages of this book, you will have an opportunity to create your own critique.

Look for the Guides

Throughout the chapters that analyze the works, thesis statements have been highlighted. The box next to the thesis helps explain what questions are being raised about the work. Supporting arguments have been underlined. The boxes next to the arguments help explain how these points support the thesis. Look for these guides throughout each critique.

Tim Burton has become one of the best known directors in Hollywood.

2

A Closer Look at
Tim Burton

Born on August 25, 1958, in Burbank, California,
Tim Burton was the older of two sons in a lower-
middle-class family. Growing up, Tim was an
introvert and did not feel comfortable in his
suburban surroundings. He spent much of his youth
listening to punk music and watching weird horror
movies. Some of his favorites were *The Brain that
Wouldn't Die*, *Frankenstein*, and *Godzilla*. Tim also
especially loved the films of Vincent Price.

Tim started making movies with a Super 8
camera with his friends in middle school and
experimented with stop-motion animation, a
style that he perfected later. Tim did not excel in
traditional academics, but his artistic talent surfaced
early on. Winning a poster design contest and
making money painting decorations for Christmas

and Halloween on his neighbors' windows,
Tim grew up developing his talent. Later, when
Burton was 18, he received a scholarship from the
California Institute of the Arts (CalArts).

Working for Disney

After going through a Disney training program
at CalArts, Burton took a job with Disney in 1979
as an animator for the movie *The Fox and the
Hound*. He then became a concept artist but did
not see many of his concepts used in films. His
vision was deemed too dark for Disney's style. But
in 1982, he got a chance to create *Vincent*, a stop-
motion animation short film about a seven-year-old
boy who imagines that he is Vincent Price. The
short film has a dark style that gives it a creepy,
gothic feel that would become Burton's signature. It
garnered awards at various film festivals.

Of the next few short films that Burton made, the
most notable is *Frankenweenie* (1984), a story about
young Victor Frankenstein, who revives his dead pet
dog. Like *Vincent*, Burton based the main character
off his own childhood. However, *Frankenweenie*
was shelved in 1984, only to have a limited release
before *Batman Returns* came out in 1992.

Making a Name for Himself

After leaving Disney, Burton made his first feature film, *Pee-wee's Big Adventure* (1985), starring Pee-wee Herman (Paul Reubens), who later hosted the television version of the film called *Pee-wee's Playhouse*. The film was a box-office hit and formed Burton's reputation as a commercial filmmaker.

Despite the unusual storyline of a house haunted by a wacky dead couple, Burton's next film, *Beetlejuice* (1988), was an even bigger success with a total gross of $73 million. It won an Oscar for best makeup and introduced Burton's unusual film aesthetic to a wider audience.

Then came Burton's biggest commercial success yet—*Batman* (1989). Though there was much conflict during production, *Batman* opened in record-breaking fashion. It was the first film to gross more than $100 million in the first ten days after it hit theaters. It was the highest-grossing film in 1989.

If *Batman* defined Burton as a commercial filmmaker, his next film, *Edward Scissorhands* (1990), defined him as an artistic filmmaker. Going back to the dark, weird aesthetic of *Vincent*, this film offered one of the most original characters in all of film. An artificially created human being, completely formed except for his hands, Edward is befriended by a suburban wife and brought to her community. The film was also Burton's first collaboration with Johnny Depp, who he would work with again throughout his career.

In the next few years, the success of Burton's films varied. While *Batman Returns* (1992) was darker and more Burton-like, it did not garner as much enthusiasm as *Batman*. Although a critical success, *Ed Wood* (1994) was Burton's first box-office failure. In the intervening years, Burton produced *Tim Burton's The Nightmare Before Christmas* (1993), a stop-animation feature film.

After producing a third Batman film, *Batman Forever* (1995), Burton returned to directing with *Mars Attacks!* (1996) and *Sleepy Hollow* (1999). Although starring many popular actors, *Mars Attacks!* came out to mixed reviews and lukewarm box-office results. *Sleepy Hollow*, starring Johnny Depp, is an unusual period-film adaptation of Washington Irving's story "The Legend of the Sleepy Hollow." The film received excellent reviews.

Burton continued to produce new work into the 2000s. He directed *Planet of the Apes* (2001), *Big Fish* (2003), *Charlie and the Chocolate Factory* (2005), *Corpse Bride* (2005), *Sweeney Todd* (2007), and *Alice in Wonderland* (2010). These films have had mixed reviews. Still, Burton possesses the unique ability to attract popular as well as critical audiences, and his indefatigable work ethic tells audiences that there is much more to come.

Burton has worked on many films with actor Johnny Depp, *right.*

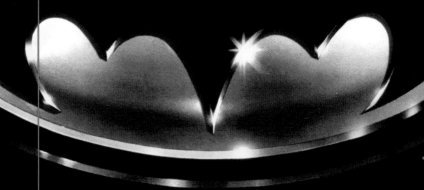

Batman hit theaters in 1989.

3

An Overview of
Batman

Batman opens to Gotham City at night. A father, a mother, and their young son try to catch a cab in the busy city. They decide to walk and find themselves in a dark alley. Suddenly, someone strikes the father, and two men rob him. Batman appears, beats up the robbers, and commands, "Tell all your friends about me. . . . I'm Batman."[1]

The mayor of Gotham City pledges to drive out crime, and he points out two men who will be responsible for this task: Harvey Dent, the district attorney, and James Gordon, the police commissioner. Watching this announcement on television is Jack Napier, second to Carl Grissom, the crime boss of the city. Napier is having an affair with Grissom's mistress, Alicia Hunt. Hunt worries Grissom will find out, but Napier is not worried.

At the scene of the robbery, reporter Alexander Knox asks Lieutenant Max Eckhardt questions about Batman. Knox says, "They say he can't be killed . . . drinks blood. . . . Is he on the police payroll?"[2] Eckhardt evades Knox's questions and goes off to meet Napier. Eckhardt turns out to be a crooked cop paid by Grissom, but he does not want to take orders from Napier.

The Birth of the Joker

Knox's story on Batman is going nowhere, but he finds a partner in Vicki Vale, a photographer interested in capturing Batman's image. To get information on Batman, they meet up with Commissioner Gordon at a benefit thrown by Bruce Wayne, a wealthy businessman. Vale and Knox get no information about Batman, but they meet Wayne, who is immediately interested in Vale. Gordon leaves the benefit after hearing about Napier's plan to clean out Axis Chemicals; Grissom has set Napier up for the cops. Wayne follows.

The police are at the plant to get Napier, and Gordon and Batman also show up. While running away from the police, Napier meets Batman, but he manages to kill Eckhardt. A fight ensues between

Napier and Batman, and Napier falls into a vat of chemicals. From this accident, Napier is disfigured, and his plastic surgery goes awry. He is left with a freakish white face in a perpetual smile. He has become the Joker.

The Joker, in his newfound identity, heartlessly murders Grissom and some of his unruly business associates and takes over his business. Sensing that Batman is a threat, the Joker seeks information on him and chances upon a photograph of Vale. He is immediately drawn to her. In the meantime, Vale and Wayne have become close, but Wayne is acting standoffish. Puzzled by his behavior, Vale tries to learn more about him, but no information surfaces. One day, she trails him and sees him leaving two red roses on the street by a run-down hotel. Curious, Vale asks Knox to research the location.

Meanwhile, mysterious deaths surface in the city. The Joker comes on television promoting his brand of everyday items such as food, alcohol, and beauty products. These items, however, cause an allergic reaction; users develop a permanent happy face and die. The products themselves are not poisonous, so the authorities are confused about the true source of the problem.

Pretending to be Wayne, the Joker lures Vale to a museum. While waiting at a table, she receives a gift box with a gas mask inside. Soon, a purple gas seeps into the museum and kills everyone except Vale who is wearing the gas mask. When the gas has dissipated, the Joker and his gang appear with loud music and paint, and they deface the art in the museum. The Joker asks Vale to photograph his "homicidal art."[3] Then when Alicia Hunt comes over wearing a mask, the Joker says that she, like him, is a "living work of art."[4] With the mask removed, Vale sees the horrifying sight of Hunt's face, which is burned and terribly disfigured.

The Joker tries to spray a chemical on Vale's face, but Batman shows up and rescues her. They escape in his Batmobile, but a car chase ensues. The Batmobile gets stuck in traffic, forcing Batman and Vale to take off on foot. When Batman is engaged in a fight against the Joker's minions, Vale snaps photographs of him. After the fight, Batman and Vale rush to Batman's secret lair. Batman says the Joker's products cause a reaction when they are mixed in a particular combination. He tells Vale to take the information to the press. Vale then wakes in her house without her film. She takes the information to the newspaper, and the press announces Batman's discovery.

Wayne Is Batman

After neglecting her for days, Wayne goes to see Vale. He tries to tell her he is Batman, but the Joker shows up. The Joker tells Vale that Hunt threw herself out the window. When he sees Wayne, the Joker points a gun at him, saying, "Have you ever danced with the devil in the pale moonlight?"[5] He shoots at Wayne and leaves, but Wayne blocked the bullet with a tray.

Vale finds out that Wayne's parents were murdered at the place where he left the roses. Through a flashback sequence, we learn that the murderer of Wayne's parents recited the line that the Joker said to Wayne. Wayne realizes that his parents' murderer may be the Joker.

The Joker sends a message through the media that he is not a killer. He says he will throw a party and dump $20 million in cash on the crowd at midnight. He then says Batman is the real terrorist and calls for a one-on-one battle with Batman.

Vale arrives at Wayne's lair and he tells her about his double life. Vale is troubled by this knowledge.

Although they confirm their love for each other, Wayne says he needs to continue to fight crime. He then goes to Axis Chemicals and blows it up.

The Final Showdown

As promised, the Joker's street party begins. He appears on a giant float and throws money into the crowd. Elated, people grab at the money and gather around the float. Batman appears in the sky in his Batmobile. The Joker then releases toxic chemicals into the air from giant balloons; Batman counteracts by snipping off the giant balloons. The Joker then shoots down the Batmobile, but Batman survives.

The Joker quickly abducts Vale and takes her to the top of a cathedral, with Batman following. When Batman reaches the top, the Joker is dancing with Vale, who is trying to break away. After Batman successfully fights off the Joker's men, he meets the Joker face-to-face. The Joker sneers at him, saying, "You made me. . . . You dropped me into that vat of chemicals."[6] The Joker's gang appears in a helicopter to lift the Joker up to safety. While the Joker is climbing the ladder of the helicopter, Batman throws his rope and catches his leg, causing the Joker to fall to his death.

With the Joker out of the picture, the city
officials hold a press conference announcing that
crimes have come to an end in Gotham City. Knox
is still after Batman's picture, but Vale seems to
be no longer interested. Batman has sent a letter to
Gotham saying that if the city needs him again, it
should flash the Batman symbol in the sky. After
the letter is read, Vale goes to meet Wayne. Wayne's
butler Alfred picks her up saying that Wayne might
be a bit late. The film ends with an image of Batman
standing beneath the shining bat sign.

Batman and the
Joker face off.

The Joker's cheerful appearance is the opposite of his true personality.

How to Apply Cultural Criticism to *Batman*

What Is Cultural Criticism?

A cultural critic considers art a product of its culture, not just a creation of an individual. Art then reflects the culture from which it springs, reinforcing the culture's important beliefs and trends, or contradicting or complicating them. Either way, cultural criticism assumes that art is in constant communication with its culture. In these respects, cultural criticism emphasizes the relationship among multiple cultural products. For instance, rather than considering books and films as primary objects of study, a cultural critic may consider anything from cartoons to advertisements to music. This critical stance helps us to understand not only art, but also the culture from which it emerges.

Applying Cultural Criticism to *Batman*

During the 1980s and the early 1990s, visual culture became very important to the masses. A famous slogan by the advertisement campaign of Canon summed up the mood of the times perfectly: "Image is everything," the advertisement claimed. With the rise of MTV, a craze in bodybuilding, and mass marketing, this was a time when Americans encountered images through more mediums, and they cared more about their own images and how they were represented by their image than ever before. Burton's 1989 film, *Batman*, perfectly reflects the importance of images. Some characters are obsessed with looking good, while others are fixated on capturing the images of others. Moreover, much of the film's violence and terror is related to the business of image making. The ways in which image and image-making circulate in the film challenge the "image is everything" mentality of the 1980s and 1990s; it demonstrates the limitation of the image to convey truth and

---

Thesis Statement

After describing the culture of the 1980s and 1990s, the author offers the thesis: "The ways in which image and image-making circulate in the film challenge the 'image is everything' mentality of the 1980s and 1990s; it demonstrates the limitation of the image to convey truth and advocates a need to escape the world of images."

advocates a need to escape the world of images.

The film foregrounds the problem of capturing an image of Batman in order to bring attention to the cultural obsession with visual representation and the media's role in satisfying that obsession. Early in the film, reporter Knox arrives at a crime scene in the hopes of finding information about Batman. He has heard various rumors about him, but having no source for clear information, Knox has difficulty writing a story about Batman. It is clear that one of his problems in constructing a coherent story of Batman is his lack of visible proof of Batman's existence. This is dramatized when Knox's fellow reporters taunt him with a cartoon image of Batman, titled "Have you seen this man?"[1] The figure is a man wearing a double-breasted suit. His head is that of a furry bat, and under the sleeves, hangs a pair of wings. More than a funny episode, the cartoon image points to a need for an image of Batman. Without this image, knowing the truth about Batman seems impossible.

> **Argument One**
> The author lays the foundation of the argument with the first point: "The film foregrounds the problem of capturing an image of Batman in order to bring attention to the cultural obsession with visual representation and the media's role in satisfying that obsession."

Argument Two

The author focuses on the character Alicia Hunt to illustrate the problem of being just an image: "Through the character of Alicia Hunt, Jack Napier's girlfriend, the film presents an image of female beauty only to destroy it."

Through the character of Alicia Hunt, Jack Napier's girlfriend, the film presents an image of female beauty only to destroy it. Hunt is played by Jerry Hall, a popular supermodel and the personification of the image-based culture of the era. The first time we see Hunt in the film is through two photographs of her hung on adjacent walls. The camera moves back to reveal two more photographs of Hunt on the right. When we finally see Hunt herself, she is blond

Hunt is presented as an image rather than a person.

and beautiful, immaculately dressed and made
up. This series of shots emphasizes the image
before the real person. That is, the film shows
photographs of Hunt before showing Hunt herself.
This fully characterizes Hunt as an image. When
Napier becomes the Joker, Hunt also transforms.
In the same room where the above sequence takes
place, she appears wearing a hideous mask. In a
later scene, we see why she is wearing a mask; her
face now is hideously burned and
disfigured. The film shows that
images are vulnerable; they can
be defaced and destroyed.

The character Vicki Vale also
fits the image of female beauty,
but her agency as a creator of
images and her intellectual
curiosity extend her beyond
her visual representation. The
sequence that introduces Vale interestingly sets up
this representation. The first shot of Vale shows only
her slim legs, crossed and raised on a table. This
is also all that reporter Knox sees, since her upper
body is hidden behind a spread newspaper. His
greeting to her is "Hello legs!" marking her identity

> **Argument Three**
> The next point offers a
> counter to the previous point:
> "The character Vicki Vale
> also fits the image of female
> beauty, but her agency as
> a creator of images and
> her intellectual curiosity
> extend her beyond her visual
> representation."

by her ideal body part.[2] For this moment, she does not seem any different from Hunt. However, when Vale is fully revealed, she is different from what the viewer has most likely expected. She is wearing heavy glasses with her hair pulled back, and she is wearing a conservative, all-black suit. We find out that she is a photographer. While the first shot presents Vale as only an image of female beauty, she turns out to be a creator of images. Her continual work in investigation and photography speaks to her being more than just an image.

The Joker, whose outward image is the opposite of his inward evil, represents the ultimate failure of images to convey truth. When we first meet Jack Napier, he is characterized as a man who cares about looking good. After Napier's botched plastic surgery, however, he is forced to wear an image insidiously contrary to his character. The scene of the Joker's reveal emphasizes the horror of this new image. When the Joker goes to pay back Grissom for setting him up, we first see him as a shadow. He stands in the

> **Argument Four**
> The author builds on the analyses of Hunt and Vale by discussing the most image-conscious character of the film, the Joker, and arguing: "The Joker, whose outward image is the opposite of his inward evil, represents the ultimate failure of images to convey truth."

doorway to Grissom's office, backlit; his shape is highlighted but invisible. He starts moving toward Grissom, but the sequence cuts to another shot, this time from Napier's back, showing the outline of his head and shoulders. When he finally becomes visible, he takes off his hat and announces his new name as the Joker. We see that his face is set in a permanent smile, his skin white, and his hair green. He tells Grissom, "I'm a lot happier," but he simultaneously kills him.[3] He even kills in a clownish way, swinging his shooting arm, turning around, squatting and standing as if he's doing a dance. When he runs out of bullets, he laughs, puts his hands up in the air, and says, "What a day!"[4] This sequence highlights the contradiction between the Joker's appearance and his violent, psychotic nature. This character is sinister, because he is not what he appears to be; his image is the opposite of who he truly is.

Batman's ability to avoid being photographed demonstrates the importance of escaping the world of images. Despite people's curiosity about Batman and his true identity, he is never

> **Argument Five**
> The author offers the final point that Batman remains a hero, because he "escapes the world of images."

photographed. Although Vale managed to take some photographs of him, Batman took the film away and avoided becoming an image. The film ends with no one having taken a photograph of Batman. However, the people of Gotham do learn the truth about Batman: he is a force of good, he is a friend, and he will continue to fight crime. At the end of the film, Batman gives the people a symbol of the bat for them to flash when they need him. This bat symbol functions as an alternative to a more recognizable image. By not becoming an image that hides and distorts truths, he continues to be meaningful in Gotham City.

Conclusion
The author restates the thesis and ponders the film's message that "image is nothing."

Burton's *Batman* reflects and critiques the image-conscious culture of the 1980s and 1990s by revealing the artificiality and distortion inherent in an image. Burton creates a terrifying world in which images are desired and created but also disfigured and destroyed. The villain, the Joker, embodies the ultimate lie of the mantra "Image is everything." In his case, image is not everything. In the character, a cultural anxiety is actualized: there is no truth in image, that image is nothing.

Thinking Critically about *Batman*

Now it is your turn to assess the critique. Consider these questions:

1. Do you agree that *Batman* responds to ideas about image in the culture of the 1980s and 1990s? Why or why not?

2. Can you think of any scenes that should be added to the author's argument? What scenes? How would they help prove the argument?

3. What other ways does *Batman* reflect the culture in which it was produced?

Other Approaches

You have read an essay that applies cultural criticism to the film *Batman* in one particular way. Are there other ways you can apply this critical approach? You might begin by researching the 1980s and 1990s to look for other cultural connections. Below are two other ways to apply cultural criticism to *Batman*.

MTV and the Joker

The Joker is an unusual, evil character because he also claims to love having fun: dancing, joking, and partying all the time. It is notable that the Joker and his gang are like a music star and his posse. In fact, in a number of scenes, one of the Joker's workers carries a boom box (a familiar image in MTV videos of the time), and they stroll as if they are in a music video. How might we interpret these references to the culture of music, fun, dance, and partying?

A thesis that responds to the above questions could be: Burton critiques the superficial gaiety of the MTV culture as hiding the more serious problems of our society, such as crime and psychological trauma.

Media and Public Opinion

Burton's *Batman* shows the ways in which the media forms public opinion. From press conferences to newspaper articles to commercials, various engines of the media form notions about Gotham City, Batman, and the Joker. It seems clear that the culture of a place, then, is largely defined by the media and practiced by the people in consensus.

A thesis that addresses this issue is: Although the media in Burton's *Batman* often disseminates wrong information, it is also a powerful engine that brings people together to fight injustice.

Edward Scissorhands

An Overview of
Edward Scissorhands

The film begins with a door opening into an archaic mansion, and the opening credits run as the camera moves into the building, up the stairs, past bizarre machinery and contraptions, and stops at a pair of white hands leading up to a shot of a mysterious old man with his eyes closed.

After the credits end, we see the mansion far away from a window of a room inhabited by an old woman and her granddaughter. The child asks, "Why is it snowing? Where did it come from?" And the grandmother begins a story with "scissors . . . a man who had scissors for hands . . . scissorhands."[1] She tells of an inventor who lived in the mansion on the hill. He created a man who was completely flesh and blood except for his hands. The inventor was old and died before he finished. The created man was "incomplete and all alone. . . . His name was Edward."[2]

Edward Finds a New Home

Walking among pastel houses of a suburb, Peg, the Avon lady, visits the neighbors to sell cosmetics. She decides to visit the dark mansion on the hill. When no one answers the door, she lets herself into the house. This is the same place shown in the opening credits. She passes strange machines covered in cobwebs. She then goes upstairs, where she sees a person in the far corner of the room: Edward Scissorhands. When Peg tries to leave, he tells her not to go, saying, "I'm not finished."[3]

Peg brings Edward to her home. He is fascinated by everything he sees, especially the pictures of Peg's family: Bill, her husband; Kevin, her son; and Kim, her daughter. Edward is especially mesmerized by Kim in the photos. But Edward has difficulty adjusting to his new surroundings at first. The next day, Edward goes outside and begins trimming the hedges. In no time, he sculpts a dinosaur and Peg's whole family.

Since the moment Edward appeared in Peg's car, the neighbors have been buzzing about him.

They pester Peg to host a barbecue to introduce her strange guest. Not everyone is welcoming, however. One neighbor, a religious fanatic, stops by to say that Edward is from hell, that the power of Satan is in him. But another neighbor, Joyce, responds to the charge that Edward is a "perversion of nature" by saying, "Why, isn't that exciting!"[4]

As Peg and Edward get ready for the party, Edward is reminded of his past by the whirring of an automatic can opener. A flashback sequence shows an assembly line of robots making cookies. An old man emerges among the machinery, takes one heart-shaped cookie and places it on the bosom of a robot.

At the party, the neighbors marvel at all that Edward can do, from playing rock, paper, scissors to sculpting beautiful figures. Edward retires for the night after the party but thinks about his father again. In another flashback, we see Edward's father giving him etiquette lessons. His father then reads him poetry and tells Edward to smile. Edward does so, but awkwardly.

Edward finally meets Kim and becomes more adjusted in his new environment. He also discovers his ability to groom pets and to cut women's hair.

The whole neighborhood seems impressed by his talents. People line up for Edward's services.

Edward's Downfall

Edward goes on a television show and gets a suggestion that he should open his own salon. Edward and Joyce go to see a vacant beauty shop, and Joyce tries to seduce him. Frightened, Edward flees. Joyce thinks that Edward has spurned her and gets angry. Edward then tries to get a loan from a bank, but he fails.

Jim, Kim's boyfriend, convinces Kim to ask Edward to help him break into the room where his father keeps valuables. Edward agrees and unlocks the door of the room. But as soon as he goes in, the door shuts behind him, setting off the alarm. Scared, Jim leaves and forcibly takes Kim with him, and Edward is trapped in the room. The police arrive and take Edward to the police station. Peg and Bill think Edward tried to steal money for the salon, because Edward does not tell anyone what happened. Edward comes back home, but the neighbors start turning against him, now listening to the religious fanatic. They decide to ostracize the family by not attending Peg's Christmas party.

Edward is clearly hurt by what happened and tells Kim that he knew what was going on but broke into the room for Kim. Then Jim shows up. Kim tells Jim to tell the truth, but he refuses. Edward begins to get angry; he starts ripping curtains, scraping the walls, and tearing the wallpaper. In the meantime, gossip mounts, with people saying that Edward attacked Joyce.

Despite the neighbors' plan to slight Peg's family, the family prepares for the party. While Kim helps Peg decorate the tree, she sees Edward sculpting a figure from a large block of ice. The ice shavings fall like snow, and Kim dances beneath the falling ice with wonder and joy. Jim appears suddenly, which startles Edward and makes him turn around and accidentally cut Kim. Jim pushes Edward out of the yard, accusing him of hurting Kim—"you can't touch anything without destroying it"— and calling him a "freak."[5] Kim tells Jim she no longer loves him and asks him to leave. Edward disappears down the street, and Bill goes out to find him. Full of anger, Edward tears at his clothes, chops off his hedge sculptures, punctures tires, and leaves a frightening sculpture in front of the fanatic's house. The police come seeking Edward.

Edward comes home to Kim, who tells him to hold her, but Edward says he cannot as he does not know what to do with his hands. Kim then goes to him and embraces him. We go to a flashback of Edward's father presenting him with hands for Christmas. Edward, excited, looks at the hands, puts his scissorhands next to them, and imagines them replaced by the real hands, but suddenly, his father drops to the floor. Edward destroys the hands as they are plunged into his blades during his father's fall. When he touches his father's face, he cuts him and gets blood on his blades.

After drinking, Jim's friend drives his van to Kim's house. Kevin, who was walking back from a friend's house, does not see the van coming toward him, but Edward sees it and pushes Kevin out of the way. Worried about Kevin's well-being, Edward fusses over him and accidentally nicks him. Then the others who come near him also get cut. Jim attacks Edward, and Edward defends himself by cutting Jim. As the police siren sounds, Kim tells Edward to run, and Edward flees to his mansion.

The people go after Edward. Kim goes up to the mansion before the others and sees that Edward is worried about Kevin. Then Jim shows up with a gun and fires at Edward. After a struggle, Edward pierces his blade into Jim and pushes him out the window, killing him. The neighbors show up, and Kim and Edward say good-bye. Kim kisses Edward and says she loves him. Edward looks astonished. Kim goes down and tells the people that Edward is dead, showing them an old part resembling Edward's hand. The people go back home.

The film returns to the opening scene of the grandmother and the granddaughter. The old woman says she "never saw him again."[6] In the background, there is snow falling. Then we see Edward in his garden, surrounded by beautiful hedge sculptures. When the girl asks if he is alive, the grandmother says that she is not sure but that she believes he is. She says, "You see, before he came down here, it never snowed. And afterwards, it did. If he weren't up there now, I don't think it would be snowing. Sometimes you can still catch me dancing in it."[7] We see Edward in his upstairs room working on numerous ice sculptures resembling Kim, children, and birds. The ice shavings fall outside, and we get a shot of the young Kim dancing in them.

Burton on the set of *Edward Scissorhands*

How to Apply Biographical Criticism to *Edward Scissorhands*

What Is Biographical Criticism?

Biographical criticism assumes that there is a critical link between an author's, or director's, life and his or her art. The critic considers various aspects of the director's identity such as his or her class, gender, race, ethnicity, and sexual orientation. Often, these identity positions lead to important struggles in the director's life. The specific time and place of the director's life may also be important factors. Finally, the critic may look to the art for the director's hidden anxieties or beliefs, unspoken hopes or desires.

Applying Biographical Criticism to *Edward Scissorhands*

Burton grew up in Burbank, California, a lower-middle-class suburb. In his biography,

Burton reveals that he did not feel he belonged in his community when he was growing up. As a result, he was "moderately destructive" and "would seek refuge from his surroundings in the movie theatre or sit in front of the television watching horror movies."[1] The setting of *Edward Scissorhands* mirrors Burton's hometown, and "it's easy to see the young, introverted Tim Burton" in its main character.[2] Although the adult Burton has achieved great success as a filmmaker, a biographical analysis of the film suggests that he still feels like an outsider. However, the fact that Edward continues to create art suggests that Burton sees the artist as ultimately a lonely figure and isolation as a necessary component of artistic creation.

Edward's traumatic past and fatherless state mirror Burton's difficult childhood. The mansion in which Edward has been living provides a window

---

Thesis Statement
The author offers a two-part thesis that Burton "still feels like an outsider" and that "Burton sees the artist as ultimately a lonely figure and isolation as a necessary component of artistic creation."

Argument One
The author makes the first point: "Edward's traumatic past and fatherless state mirror Burton's difficult childhood" and analyzes Edward's mansion as a window into his past.

into Edward's terrifying past. When Peg enters, we see the house as dark, empty, and eerie. One can extend this interpretation to Edward. There is something traumatic in his past. This becomes clear when we learn about Edward's dead father and his incomplete transformation. This dark mood of the mansion is most evident in the upstairs room. The ceiling has a giant hole, suggesting violence. We also see various items pasted on the wall: pictures of beautiful bodies, an article about a boy born without eyes, a picture of Mary and baby Jesus. These items suggest Edward's psychological anxiety about his body and parentage. The carefully constructed setting of Edward's mansion alludes to his traumatic past filled with solitude and confusion. Although not to the same degree, Burton also had a sad childhood. As one biographer wrote, Burton was a "lonely little boy who was ignored by the people around him."[3]

The setting of the rest of the film, the US suburb of the mid-twentieth century, emphasizes uniformity and conformity—why Burton found his childhood suburban home so oppressive.

> **Argument Two**
> The author's next point identifies the suburban setting of the film, echoing Burton's childhood home, as a place of "uniformity and conformity."

Juxtaposed against Edward's crumbling mansion is the neat suburban community where Peg lives. The pastel houses are indistinguishable from one another. The uniform setting of the suburb goes hand in hand with the way people behave. When someone spots Edward riding in Peg's car, word gets around and almost all the women in the town congregate to figure out who Edward is. There seems to be no individuality in the suburb; all are interested in the same thing. Furthermore, the lives of the people in the suburb are so set that the women all gather on the streets to talk about Edward, then all the husbands come home from work, and then all the women scatter to return to their homes probably to return to their domestic responsibilities. At the beginning of a day, the men come out of their houses one by one. Then we see the cars drive away, presumably taking the men to work.

Argument Three
The author continues to discuss the suburb but emphasizes the community's ultimate rejection of difference.

Edward, like Burton who was an "alienated suburban child," does not fit in; the suburban community initially finds his difference exotic but ultimately unacceptable.[4] The women of the suburb are initially hyperexcited about Edward's peculiarities. They practically barge in on Peg to meet her strange visitor. At the party, the neighbors praise many of Edward's talents, such as using his hands to grill and making hedge sculptures. As an explicit statement of acceptance, a war veteran with a steel limb tells him, "Don't let anyone tell you that you have a handicap."[5] Prompting female neighbor Joyce to add, "You're not handicapped . . . you're exceptional."[6] As quickly as the neighbors started buzzing around Edward, however, they turn against him. They become suspicious of Edward, and eventually hate him. This change in public opinion shows that the people's initial interest was a temporary fascination with the exotic rather than a true acceptance of differences.

While Edward is marked by his differences, he is presented as an artist; his gardens, haircuts, and ice sculptures have the power to inspire and to move people. From early on, Edward is clearly presented with artistic talent. When he is sculpting or cutting hair, he looks completely

> **Argument Four**
> The author begins to argue the second part of the thesis: "While Edward is marked by his differences, he is presented as an artist; his gardens, haircuts, and ice sculptures have the power to inspire and to move people."

At first, Edward's neighbors appreciate his artistic talents.

absorbed in his work. When he first discovers his ability to trim dog fur, he stares intensely at his work with various emotions, and when he is finished, he looks satisfied with his creation. When he cuts Joyce's hair for the first time, he takes her head in his hands, moves it slightly here and there, looks at it from various angles and gets to work. He then proceeds to cut other women's hair and produces unconventional cuts, clearly a result of his momentary inspiration and artistic sensibility. Through his art, Edward inspires others. Toward the end of the film, Edward creates an ice sculpture. He stands on top of a ladder sculpting a figure twice his height. Kim's dancing under the falling ice particles shows the affect of Edward's art, that it can move people, give people joy, and create the impossible (in Southern California, there is no snow).

Edward's final isolation is unfortunate, but the film suggests that he continues to create art that affects subsequent generations. As more people make him out to be a menace, they go after him in mob fashion. Furthermore, Jim's persistence to punish Edward forces Edward to strike back and kill him. This leaves Kim with no other choice but to lie and say that Edward is dead, dooming Edward to isolation. However, rather than living a life of darkness, we see Edward in the final moments of the film living a creative life. He is in his garden in broad daylight. The flowers are in colorful bloom, surrounded by Edward's magnificent hedge sculptures. Then when we move upstairs; we don't see the cold, empty room that we had seen earlier. Instead, ice sculptures of various shapes: a woman resembling Kim, children playing,

> **Argument Five**
> The author builds on the previous paragraph by exploring the connection between isolation and sustained artistic power. She asserts: "Edward's final isolation is unfortunate, but the film suggests that he continues to create art that affects subsequent generations."

and birds at a fountain decorate the space. These are noticeable shapes from Edward's experience in the world of other people. Through his art, he is able to remember and to relive that experience. Furthermore, we see that he is not creating the sculpture just for himself; the ice shavings from his sculpting are flowing out of his windows into the world as snow. Kim says that it started snowing after Edward went back, and she adds, "Sometimes you can still catch me dancing in it."[7] While it is unfortunate that Edward remains isolated in the end, at least this way, he can be as creative as he likes, giving people snow, giving people joy.

> **Conclusion**
> The author restates the thesis and offers a final reflection on Edward and Burton as solitary artists.

If we read Edward Scissorhands as Tim Burton's double, we can see the ways in which Burton's eccentricity and the monotonous suburban life still haunt him. However, his success as a filmmaker and his continual output parallels Edward's artistic life. Edward's isolation perhaps suggests that Burton does not quite feel like he belongs, but at the same time, it could be this uniqueness that leads to his inspirational films.

Thinking Critically about *Edward Scissorhands*

Now it is your turn to assess the critique.
Consider these questions:

1. Do you agree that *Edward Scissorhands* reflects Burton's childhood? Why or why not?

2. What parts of the author's argument were the strongest? Which were the weakest? What could the author add to her argument to make it more convincing?

3. How does this understanding of Burton's childhood influence your views on his other films? Do you think it makes sense to try to understand a filmmaker through his or her work?

Other Approaches

You have read an essay that applies biographical criticism to the film *Edward Scissorhands* in one particular way. Are there other ways you can apply this critical approach? Begin by thinking about other aspects of Burton's biography that connect to the film.

Parents and Children

Not only did Burton generally have an unhappy childhood, he also did not always live with his parents. He lived with his grandmother between 12 to 16 years of age and later lived in a small apartment above her garage, paying rent by working in a restaurant after school. It seems that he might not have had consistent parental guidance in his youth.

Now consider the various parent-child relationships that exist in the film: Peg and Bill and their children Kim and Kevin; Jim and his father; and Edward and his father. A thesis that could result from this investigation is: Although Peg is a loving and accepting mother, the fathers are either ineffectual or cruel, unable to guide their children in their growth as stable adults.

Psychology of Edward/Burton

A biographical critique works with the known information about the author but also speculates about deeper, complex aspects of the author that may be hidden. Oftentimes, the critic looks to the art for insights into the artist's psychology or deep-seated beliefs that may or may not be controversial. Because Edward is such an unusual character with a traumatic history and a dark life, he offers a look into Burton's psychology.

Thinking deeply about Edward, consider the kinds of anxieties and fears that affect Edward. A thesis that delves into the psychology of Edward and Burton could be: Although Edward, like Burton, is a mild, kind person for most of the film, his insecurities about being different and his fear of abandonment come out in anger and frustration, fueling his destructive side.

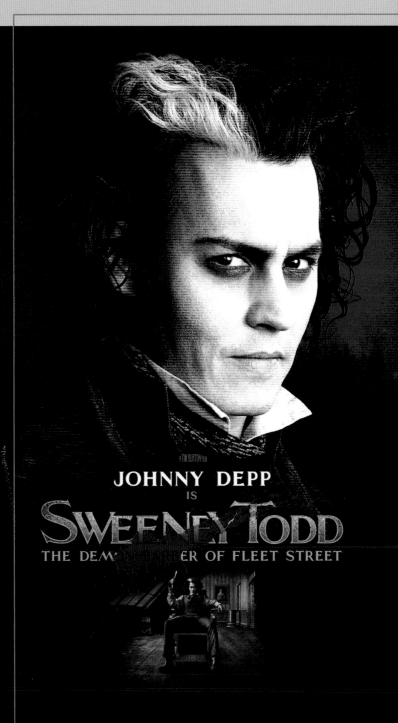

Johnny Depp stars as Sweeney Todd.

An Overview of *Sweeney Todd*

As the musical begins, a ship arrives in London, England, carrying Sweeney Todd and his young friend Anthony. They sing "No Place Like London," a song about an unhappy reunion. The film quickly moves into a flashback, as Todd tells of an unfortunate story of a barber and his family. A judge covets the barber's wife and arranges for the barber's incarceration. The barber is taken away, leaving his wife and baby daughter. The brief tale ends as the ship docks and Todd and Anthony go their separate ways.

"The Worst Pies in London"

In London, Todd arrives at Mrs. Lovett's, a run-down shop that offers the "The Worst Pies in London," as her song describes. After this odd introduction, Todd asks about the space upstairs where he had lived with his family before he was incarcerated, and Mrs. Lovett sings "Poor Thing," which tells the story of a barber who occupied the space some time ago, the same barber that Todd spoke of earlier. This second flashback sequence tells of the judge's sexual violation of the barber's wife after the husband was put away. Todd's violent reaction to the story reveals to Mrs. Lovett that he is the barber, Benjamin Barker. Mrs. Lovett tells Todd that his wife, Lucy, poisoned herself and that his daughter is with Judge Turpin. After hearing this, Todd is more committed to his revenge. He sings the song "My Friends" to his old knives given to him by Mrs. Lovett. During the song sequence, Mrs. Lovett's feelings for Todd emerge, and Todd ends the song by raising the knife in the air, saying, "At last, my arm is complete again!"[1]

Johanna and the Pie Shop

Anthony sees Johanna, Todd's daughter, sitting at her window. The two find themselves drawn to each other, and Anthony's song "Johanna" affirms their budding love. Judge Turpin finds out about the two and strongly warns Anthony to stay away, but

Anthony vows to rescue Johanna. Johanna throws out a key for Anthony. Unfortunately, the judge witnesses this act.

In the meantime, Todd, with the help of Mrs. Lovett, establishes a reputation as the best barber on Fleet Street. In the marketplace, they attend a sales demonstration put on by Pirelli, the self-proclaimed best barber, and his boy assistant Toby. Todd challenges and beats Pirelli in a shaving duel, gaining the attention of Beadle Bamford, Judge Turpin's right-hand man.

Planning out his revenge, Todd waits impatiently for Beadle to come to his shop, but instead, it is Pirelli who shows up. When Todd realizes that Pirelli knows his true identity, Todd brutally kills Pirelli. Toby is suspicious at Pirelli's sudden disappearance, but he is distracted by Mrs. Lovett's offer of food and drink. She later asks him to work at her bakery.

The judge visits Todd's barbershop to improve his physical appearance for Johanna, whom he is now planning to marry. Shocked but excited at seeing Turpin, Todd seats him down and relaxes him by chatting about women. They sing the song "Pretty Women" together, as Todd prepares himself

Working again as a barber, Todd craves revenge.

to kill Turpin. A moment before Todd plans to cut Turpin, Anthony comes in to tell Todd about his plan to rescue Johanna. The judge, learning of the alliance, leaves in a fury, foiling Todd's plan for revenge.

While Todd broods in frustration, the ever-practical Mrs. Lovett searches for a solution for the dead body of Pirelli and arrives at an ingenious idea—to use the dead body as an ingredient for her pies. They sing the song "A Little Priest," which lays out the dark plan: they will kill whomever they can for the business and fool their town into cannibalism. Todd then designs a mechanism for mass murder. The people he kills would be sent down through a chute, which opens under the barber chair. In the basement, the bodies would be dismembered and meat put into a grinder for the pies.

Soon, Todd finds himself knee-deep in the murdering business, but Mrs. Lovett's secret recipe works! The pie shop begins to thrive. With more money, Mrs. Lovett begins to dream of a normal, happy life for her, Todd, and Toby. But Todd continues to dream of revenge, oblivious to Mrs. Lovett's feelings.

The Showdown

After discovering Anthony and Johanna's plan of escape, Turpin sends Johanna to an asylum for the mentally ill. Todd helps Anthony by suggesting that Anthony disguise himself as a wigmaker's apprentice and enter the asylum. The plan is successful, and he rescues Johanna. In the meantime, Todd manages to lure Turpin to his shop by promising him the young couple.

While Todd prepares his second attempt at revenge, complications arise. Toby, who is getting more attached to Mrs. Lovett, becomes suspicious

Mrs. Lovett falls
in love with Todd.

of Todd and begins to worry about Mrs. Lovett's
well-being. He sings the song "Not While I'm
Around," declaring his loyalty to her. Toby then
sees Mrs. Lovett with the dead Pirelli's purse and
becomes even more suspicious. Not wanting her
and Todd's scheme to be exposed, Mrs. Lovett locks
Toby in the basement, where he shockingly finds
human body parts. Mrs. Lovett and Todd come after
Toby, but he is nowhere to be found.

Meanwhile, Anthony and Johanna arrive at
the shop, and Johanna, left alone for some time by
Anthony, looks at photos and Todd's implements
without knowing that Todd is her father. Suddenly,

a beggar comes into the shop, and Johanna quickly hides in a trunk. Todd comes up and sees the beggar, and at the same time, hears the judge's voice. Intent on carrying out his revenge, Todd quickly kills the beggar and sends her down the chute. When Turpin arrives, he is finally able to get his revenge. As they once again sing "Pretty Women," Todd reveals his true identity. At the moment of recognition, Todd violently kills Turpin and sends him down the chute. Todd then discovers Johanna but does not recognize her in male disguise. Alarmed by Mrs. Lovett's shriek from down below, he lets Johanna go.

Todd goes down and helps Mrs. Lovett dispose of the judge's body. As he turns to leave, he seems to recognize the dead beggar he just killed. When he looks at her closely, he sees that she is his wife, Lucy. Mrs. Lovett had lied to Todd about Lucy because of her feelings for him. Lucy took poison but did not die; she only lost her sanity. In his rage, Todd kills Mrs. Lovett by pushing her into the oven. As Todd holds Lucy's dead body and grieves, Toby, who had been hiding in the sewers, grabs Todd's knife on the floor and cuts Todd's throat. The film ends with an image of Todd with Lucy in his arms, his pouring blood dripping onto her limp body.

Todd focuses more on revenge than justice.

How to Apply Marxist Criticism to *Sweeney Todd*

What Is Marxist Criticism?

Marxist criticism is based on the idea that the modern, capitalistic society operates under an unequal class system, with the working class on the bottom and the bourgeoisie, or those who control economic, social, and cultural aspects of the society, on top. Seeing the society from this perspective, the Marxist critic analyzes how classes are formed and how differences between them are maintained. This mode of criticism also looks to criticize the disparity of power between classes as well as to discover possible solutions to or effective modes of rebelling against the unequal class system. A Marxist critic is interested in empowering the lower class.

Applying Marxist Criticism to *Sweeney Todd*

Sweeney Todd begins in the night as a ship brings the central character back to London's dark streets. Todd, whose real name is Benjamin Barker, experienced ruin at the hands of Judge Turpin, who framed and incarcerated Barker, sexually violated and discarded Barker's wife, took their daughter into his care, and is now interested in marrying the teenage girl. This is a world where men such as Turpin can easily take from the less privileged and where men such as Barker stand defenseless. This disparity of power is clearly due to unequal class status. While the film exposes the inequality and the injustice of the class system of nineteenth-century London, its examination falls short in that Todd fails to incite a true rebellion. His indiscriminate killing is a result of his desire for personal revenge and a lack of class consciousness.

Judge Turpin and Todd are clearly set up as moral opposites

Thesis Statement

The author presents the thesis: "While the film exposes the inequality and the injustice of the class system of nineteenth-century London, its examination falls short in that Todd fails to incite a true rebellion. His indiscriminate killing is a result of his desire for personal revenge and a lack of class consciousness."

Argument One

The author offers the first point that the lower and the upper classes are "moral opposites" of good and evil, respectively.

<u>in the beginning of the film, the former abusing his power to satiate his appetite, while the latter is innocently content with his life.</u> The memory sequence that takes place in the marketplace, where the Judge first sees and covets Barker's wife, illustrates this clearly. Juxtaposed against the dark opening of the film, the sequence begins in full daylight, the family at the center of the shot, surrounded by colorful flowers of a street florist. As Todd's song describes them as "beautiful" and "virtuous," light falls directly on the family, which suggests their moral purity and goodness.[1] Juxtaposed against this happy scene, Judge Turpin appears from the shadows; he remains mostly in darkness. Through such use of lighting and scenery, the film makes a clear moral separation between the two parties.

<u>Rather than rebelling against the class system, Todd seeks personal revenge and, more disturbingly, pleasure in that revenge.</u> Before the mass murder begins, Todd manages to bring Turpin to his barbershop. After seating him, Todd tells "his

> **Argument Two**
> Here the author begins to argue that Todd does not incite a true rebellion against the upper class, since he "seeks personal revenge and more disturbingly, pleasure in that revenge."

friend" the knife to "enjoy" it and that "revenge can't be taken in haste."[2] Todd lingers in the moment too long, and is interrupted before he can finish the job. If Todd had not relished his moment of possible revenge, he might have punished Turpin quickly and moved on. If he had been more intent on meting out justice and less on his pleasure in the kill, he might have avoided the violence and the tragedy that follow. Because of this botched attempt, the film raises the possibility that it is Todd's personal desire for revenge that hinders justice being served.

> **Argument Three**
> The author points out another way in which Todd's actions are problematic: "The way in which Todd's (and Mrs. Lovett's) killing spree fails as a rebellion against the unequal class system is that it is not directed toward the upper class, those who possess and abuse power."

The film soon takes a more morbid turn as Todd and Lovett begin their mass killing. The way in which Todd's (and Mrs. Lovett's) killing spree fails as a rebellion against the unequal class system is that it is not directed toward the upper class, those who possess and abuse power. Analyzing the lyrics of the song "A Little Priest" reveals the misdirection of their violence. Piqued by Mrs. Lovett's murderous suggestion, Todd looks out the window and alerts her to "the sound of the world"—"crunching noises pervading the air" of "man devouring man"—this may be an apt description of their cruel society, but their plan only maintains the status quo, literally, by serving human meat to other humans.[3] On the surface, their plan seems political as Todd tells Mrs. Lovett, "the history of the world . . . is those below serving those up above . . . how gratifying for once to know that those above will serve those down below," but ultimately, no one is safe from their murdering hands.[4] Todd even says, they will "take the customers that [they] can get," that they'll "not discriminate great and small," that they'll serve "anyone" to "anyone at all."[5] Rather than punishing those who are taking advantage of the underprivileged, their plan is simply to create havoc even if it means punishing innocent people.

Although Todd knows that he is a victim of injustice, he does not understand the larger class system as one of inequality, where anyone in a lower class is equally or even more vulnerable. Because of this lack of understanding, he does not recognize those in a

> **Argument Four**
> The author offers the final point that Todd fails as a true rebel, because "he does not understand the larger class system as one of inequality, where anyone in a lower class is equally or even more vulnerable."

class lower than his. His wife, as a beggar, is such a person, as is the young Toby, who had been abused in the workhouse until he met Pirelli. Because Todd and Mrs. Lovett's plan is to be indiscriminate, they are willing to punish anyone standing in their way, even those who have very limited power. Had Todd and Mrs. Lovett sympathized with the lower class, the tragedy would not have occurred. Because Todd's rebellious act is not born out of a deep understanding of the class system, he fails to enact a true rebellion against the upper class.

Conclusion
The author concludes by restating the thesis and offering a final comment.

While *Sweeney Todd* reveals the appalling wrongs of a society based on class privilege and power, it does not provide an example of how one could truly rebel against the class structure. As a primary representative of the lower class, Todd could have executed a more pointed rebellion; instead, his desire for personal revenge and lack of understanding of himself within the class system lead to his failure as a true revolutionary. Rather than threatening the system that took away everything in his life, he succumbs to the system by becoming a monster that has to be eliminated.

Thinking Critically about *Sweeney Todd*

Now it is your turn to assess the critique. Consider these questions:

1. Do you agree with the author's thesis about *Sweeney Todd*? Does Todd fail to incite a true rebellion against the corrupt upper class? Why or why not?

2. What was the strongest part of the author's argument? What was the weakest? Is there anything you would add to this critique?

3. What else might *Sweeney Todd* reveal about class struggles? Can you think of an alternative thesis using Marxist criticism?

Other Approaches

You have read an essay that applies Marxist criticism to the film *Sweeney Todd* in one particular way. Are there other ways you can apply this critical approach? Think further about how classes are defined in our society, who has power and who does not, and how the film comments on these issues.

Meaning of Work

In studying the class system, a Marxist critic might be interested in analyzing various kinds of work in our society, how they were valued and classified, and how they formed our identities in the modern world. Along these lines, you might think further about the types of work presented in the film and what they mean to individuals and the society.

Almost every character in the film works: Turpin as a judge; Todd as a barber; Mrs. Lovett as a baker; Toby as first a barber's and later a baker's assistant. A thesis that considers the relationship between these characters and work is: *Sweeney Todd* does not present work as a meaningful activity for most of the characters; it either gives them power for selfish gains or merely provides the economic means of survival.

Family and Class

One way in which the classes are differently defined revolves around the family. The film uses the family as the basis of Todd's lower-class morality. He was a good man who had a beautiful wife and a lovely daughter, and only when his family was torn apart, he became immoral. However, the upper-class Judge Turpin has no family and does not seem interested in domestic happiness. Instead, he is driven by sexual urges, later willing to use marriage for sexual conquest of a teenage girl.

Think further about how the family works to differentiate classes in the film. A thesis that addresses this issue could be: *Sweeney Todd* champions the lower class through the theme of family. The lower class characters' desire to maintain a happy domestic unit, unlike the upper-class characters' disregard for it, suggests an important way in which the lower class promotes community.

Alice in Wonderland was released in theaters in 2010.

Chapter

9

An Overview of
Alice in Wonderland

Burton's *Alice in Wonderland* begins with Alice's
father, Charles, who dreams about opening trading
posts in such faraway places as Bangkok and
Jakarta, despite his business partner telling him,
"You have finally lost your senses."[1] Charles
does not mind senselessness. But Alice worries
about nightmares of falling endlessly and meeting
odd characters such as a smiling cat. Her father
reassures her, "It's only a dream."[2]

Thirteen years later, Alice arrives at a party that
she later finds out is her own engagement party. She
is nervous, because unlike her, her suitor, Hamish,
is unimaginative. Alice does not know if she wants
to marry Hamish. Walking in the garden, Alice
sees a rabbit in a waistcoat and decides to follow it,
despite her suspicion that she is going mad. When

she catches sight of her sister's husband kissing another woman, Alice is more confused. Hamish then calls Alice over and proposes in front of all the guests. Alice hesitates, sees the rabbit again, and without answering the proposal, follows it down a hole in the ground.

A Strange Place

Alice starts to fall in what seems to be a bottomless hole. After some time, she falls through a ceiling and lands on what appears to be the floor, but it is actually the ceiling, so she lands again, now on the floor.

Alice is in a room with many doors, which she tries to open, but they are locked. She finds a key on a table that opens a tiny door, but she cannot fit through it. She takes various potions she finds in the room that change her size. Meanwhile, voices wonder whether she is the right Alice. After much size-shifting, she is finally able to fit through the door.

When Alice steps out, she finds herself in an alien world. Unrecognizable creatures fly around, and strange flowers bloom. She then meets the rabbit, Tweedledum and Tweedledee, and the Dormouse. The creatures ask her whether she

is the right Alice. Alice responds, "How can I
be the wrong Alice, when this is my dream?"[3]
Still seeking an answer, the creatures take her to
Absalom, a wise caterpillar. Absalom shows them a
compendium that records the history of this strange
place, even an episode of Alice slaying the monster
Jabberwocky. Absalom says she is "not hardly" the
right Alice, which upsets everyone.[4] Alice then tries
to wake up but cannot. Suddenly, Bandersnatch,
a large white beast appears with playing-card
soldiers and the Knave of Hearts. The Dormouse
stabs Bandersnatch's eye out right before it tries

Alice and her
new friends ask
Absalom whether
Alice is the "right
Alice."

to eat Alice. Alice runs off with Tweedledee and Tweedledum. But Tweedledee and Tweedledum are captured and taken to the Red Queen's castle.

The Knave of Hearts finds the compendium, sees what is recorded there, and takes off with his soldiers to tell the Red Queen. When the Red Queen sees the part where Alice slays the Jabberwocky, she orders the capture of Alice.

In the meantime, Alice meets the Cheshire Cat, who binds her wound from Bandersnatch and takes her to March Hare and the Mad Hatter's tea party. Excited, the Hatter tells her that she is the right Alice and serves her tea. The party is cut short when the Knave of Hearts arrives. The Mad Hatter quickly gives Alice a shrinking potion and hides her in a teapot. The three talk nonsense, sing, and giggle, which distracts the Knave and soldiers from finding Alice. After accusing them of madness, the Knave of Hearts leaves.

Alice gets on the Mad Hatter's hat, and they head for the White Queen's castle. When the Hatter recites a poem about Alice slaying the Jabberwocky with the Vorpol Sword, she says she cannot possibly do that, which disappoints him. The Hatter then says, "you've lost your muchness," points to her

heart, and adds, "in there something is missing."[5]
He goes on to relay the evil deeds of the Red
Queen. The Hatter had worked for the White Queen
when the Jabberwocky burned down the place. The
Knave of Hearts orchestrated the destruction with
the Vorpol Sword.

Alice Takes Charge

The Mad Hatter and Alice are tracked by the
Knave of Hearts. The Hatter manages to hide Alice
but cannot save himself and is taken by the playing-
card soldiers. The next day, the bloodhound Bayard
finds Alice, and tells her that Frabjous Day is near
and that she must prepare for it. Suddenly, Alice
angrily says, "This is my dream. I will decide where
it goes from here."[6] She goes to the Red Queen's
castle to rescue the Hatter.

When Alice gets to the castle, she reunites with
the rabbit and eats the magical cake that turns her
into a giant. Not knowing her identity, the Red
Queen sees Alice and welcomes her. Alice also sees
Tweedledee and Tweedledum and the Hatter.

Bayard goes to the White Queen's castle and
tells her that Alice has returned to Underland. At
the Red Queen's castle, Alice gets help from the

Mad Hatter and the rabbit to recapture the Vorpol Sword guarded by Bandersnatch. Alice befriends the creature, enabling her to get the sword.

In the meantime, the Knave of Hearts makes advances on Alice. When he is caught by the Red Queen, who loves him, he lies that Alice is obsessed with him. Furious, the Red Queen commands, "Off with her head!"[7] During the chase, Alice's identity is revealed, but Bandersnatch takes Alice away to the White Queen. Alice drinks the White Queen's potion that restores her to her normal size. Alice then goes to see Absalom and tells him, "I'm Alice, but not that one," but Absalom says, "You're almost Alice."[8] The Red Queen orders

The Red Queen orders Alice's capture and execution.

the execution of the Mad Hatter and the Dormouse,
but the execution is foiled by the Cheshire Cat.
Everyone reunites at the White Queen's castle.

Alice is unsure about fighting the Jabberwocky,
but the next day, Alice remembers that she was
there before, when she mistakenly called the place
Wonderland. Knowing that she is the real Alice,
she meets the Red Queen's army in her armor.
The Jabberwocky and Alice face off. Struggling
at first, Alice finds courage by naming all the
impossible things that are real—cats disappearing,
a place called Wonderland, and her slaying the
Jabberwocky. She and the creature go to the top of
the ruins where the battle is being held. Alice climbs
on top of the creature, but it throws her off into
the air. She comes down, however, slicing off its
head. The Red Queen and the Knave of Hearts are
chained together and banished forever. Alice goes
home.

Alice tells Hamish she cannot marry him and
tells people around her: "This is my life; I'll decide
what to do with it."[9] Alice decides to live out her
father's dream of expanding trade routes to Sumatra
and maybe even China. The film ends with Alice
aboard a ship leaving England.

Alice's journey in Underland is strange and confusing at first.

10

How to Apply Feminist Criticism to *Alice in Wonderland*

What Is Feminist Criticism?

Feminism is the belief that men and women are equally capable genders. Feminist critics look at works of art, film, literature, and even music to see how women are portrayed. Is the woman in the film independent and strong? Or does she rely on a male protagonist to rescue her or direct her? Figuring out how women are portrayed in different works of art can help us understand ideas about women in our social past and present.

Applying Feminist Criticism to *Alice in Wonderland*

Burton's *Alice in Wonderland* focuses on Alice and her identity as an adult woman. Before the film takes us to Underland, Alice receives a

Thesis Statement

In the first paragraph, the author presents the thesis: "Burton solidifies Alice's female, adult identity by developing her into an empowered woman, and, therefore, establishing the importance of female power at a young age."

Argument One

The author presents the first point: "Burton's Alice is set up with an unstable identity from the beginning of the film because she feels that she does not fit into her gender role."

proposal for marriage and is uncertain as to what she should do with her life. Burton solidifies Alice's female, adult identity by developing her into an empowered woman, and, therefore, establishing the importance of female power at a young age.

Burton's Alice is set up with an unstable identity from the beginning of the film because she feels that she does not fit into her gender role. In the film, Alice is a young woman facing important decisions in life. During the carriage ride to her engagement party with her mother, we see that Alice is uncomfortable about following rules prescribed for her. When her mother chides her for wearing neither a corset nor stockings, she responds, "Who is to say what is proper?"[1] Alice faces more serious decisions at the party. She learns that Hamish is going to propose marriage. It is clearly set up that Alice's relationship with Hamish is to be unequal.

Margaret, Alice's sister, reminds her that Hamish is a lord, and Hamish's mother tells her that she is "lovely" and will bear beautiful children.[2] The expectation that women should marry well and devote themselves to achieving domestic happiness does not sit well with Alice. So when Hamish proposes, instead of answering him, Alice follows the rabbit to Underworld.

It is clear at the beginning of the film that Alice does not yet know who she is or how she should behave. *Alice in Wonderland* emphasizes size-shifting to demonstrate Alice's unstable identity. After falling down the rabbit hole, Alice finds herself in a room with multiple doors. She finds a key and manages to open a door, but it is too small for her to walk out of. She then finds a potion and drinks it, which shrinks her. The shot places Alice next to a table, which comparatively shows Alice in relation to a stable object, creating a jarring effect. Alice emerges from a heap of her dress and runs over to the door, showing the spatial change relative

> **Argument Two**
>
> The author now focuses on how Alice's lack of identity is expressed in the film. She states: "*Alice in Wonderland* emphasizes size-shifting to demonstrate Alice's unstable identity." The author offers a close reading of Alice's beginning moments in her newfound surroundings.

to Alice's new size. Then, in an upward shot that shows Alice's view of the table now too high, we again see how the environment has changed for Alice, even though it is technically only she who has changed. Soon Alice becomes so big that her head has to bend against the ceiling. By utilizing multiple shots that show the perspective of Alice shifting and props that emphasize the changing perception of the environment, Burton shows Alice's lack of a stable identity and the jarring effects of that instability.

Burton's film focuses on the importance of Alice establishing her own identity. In the size-shifting scene discussed above, the viewer hears voices that go back and forth between her being the right and the wrong Alice. After Alice exits the room, she meets those who had been wondering about her identity: the rabbit, Tweedledee and Tweedledum, and other creatures. Questioned about her authenticity, Alice says, "How can I be the wrong Alice when this is my dream?"[3] But it is unclear whether in fact this is Alice's dream when she is

---

Argument Three

The author's next point expands the previous point by explaining how Alice's lack of identity is problematic in the film. She asserts: "Burton's film focuses on the importance of Alice establishing her own identity."

---

unable to awake from it. Still, Alice is beginning to realize that it is up to her to claim her own identity. It is, after all, *her* "dream."

But Alice's confusion about her identity again increases when she meets Absalom. He says to Alice, "The question is who are you?"[4] And when Alice says her name, he says, "We shall see."[5] Alice is perturbed and says, "What do you mean by that? I ought to know who I am."[6] Then as a response, Absalom shows her a compendium that records all the events of Underland. There is an image of Alice defeating the monster Jabberwocky, which confounds her. She says, "That's not me," and when the rabbit asks, "Is she the right Alice?" Absalom says, "not hardly," a confusing answer.[7]

Once Alice stabilizes her identity by becoming a heroine in Underland, defeating the Jabberwocky and restoring order to the land, Alice is able to reject marriage and to make herself an empowered woman of trade who extends her father's legacy. Although Alice regains her memory of her past visit

---

Argument Four

The author arrives at the heart of her argument: "Once Alice stabilizes her identity by becoming a heroine in Underland, defeating the Jabberwocky and restoring order to the land, Alice is able to reject marriage and to make herself an empowered woman of trade who extends her father's legacy."

to Underland, she is still unsure about her ability to fight the Red Queen's champion Jabberwocky on Frabjous Day. On that day, the Red Queen arrives with her knight and army and calls forth her champion. On the side of the White Queen, Alice emerges dressed in armor, carrying the Vorpol Sword, ready to battle. She battles triumphantly, decapitating the creature and bringing order to Underland. The Red Queen is banished, and the good White Queen rules again. When the Hatter suggests that she can stay in Underland, Alice replies, "There are questions I have to answer, things I have to do."[8] And surely enough, as soon as Alice returns home, she rejects the proposal. She tells her concerned sister, "This is my life; I'll decide what to do with it."[9] Indeed, she makes a decision to go into business and accepts the offer to work for Hamish's father's company. In the way the film moves quickly from the defeat of the Jabberwocky to Alice's brand-new life, we see the clear connection between Alice's heroics in Underland and her ability to shape her identity and life in the real world. Furthermore, the conflict over what a woman should be doing with her life is resolved by Alice's choices.

When she becomes the hero of Underland, Alice claims her own identity.

Alice's successful grasp of her identity at the end of the film supports the idea that young women need to make their own choices to obtain positive futures. In the final scene of the film, Alice is aboard a ship set to leave England. She is wearing a tie and coat. In dress, lifestyle

Argument Five
The author proves the last part of her thesis, focusing on how this reading relates to the viewer and society. She asserts: "Alice's successful grasp of her identity at the end of the film supports the idea that young women need to make their own choices to obtain positive futures."

choice, and following her father's legacy, Alice has become an unusual woman for the time, but she is confident and happy with her choice. Alice's visit to Underland, where she was forced to make her own decisions and claim her individual agency, leads her to a life that she appreciates. Burton's depiction of Alice suggests young women must be given an arena, like Alice's Underland, to learn about themselves and make their own decisions to be successful.

Conclusion
The conclusion restates the thesis and offers a final comment on the importance of discovering one's identity.

Burton's film poses Alice's identity crisis as a problem to be resolved and advocates that young women should be allowed to make unusual choices if those choices are right for them and not to be persuaded by those advocating for a more traditional path, if it is not the right path for them. It is a message that empowers all young people to make bold choices that can bring them ultimate meaning in life.

Thinking Critically about *Alice in Wonderland*

Now it is your turn to assess the critique.
Consider these questions:

1. Do you agree with the author's thesis about *Alice in Wonderland?* Why or why not?

2. What parts of the argument were the most convincing? Which were the weakest? How would you add to this argument?

3. What other arguments could you make about *Alice in Wonderland* using feminist criticism? What evidence would you use to support them?

Other Approaches

You have read an essay that applies feminist criticism to the film *Alice in Wonderland* in one particular way. Are there other ways you can apply this critical approach? Following are two alternative approaches.

Female Insanity

Although Alice seems to obtain a future that she will enjoy at the end of the film, it is clear that Alice is quite different from the people in the society around her. Alice herself often wonders if she is going insane in the earlier scenes of the film.

Examining the above ideas, one could arrive at the thesis: Alice's imagination and experience in Underland supports her own belief that she is going insane and, therefore, asserts that there is something mentally wrong with women who do not fit into the gender roles prescribed for them.

Alice's Age

After Alice's trip to Underland, she returns to the real world as an empowered woman. Leaving the fantasy behind, she starts a business, focusing on her career. Alice's father, however, seems to have retained his imaginative spirit even as an adult. Why does empowered Alice need to sober up and think realistically?

Along these lines, one could formulate the following thesis: The new context of Alice's life suggests that in order to be taken seriously as a woman, she needs to abandon magic and fantasy.

You Critique It

Now that you have learned about several different critical theories and how to apply them to film, are you ready to perform a critique of your own? You have read that this type of evaluation can help you look at movies from a new perspective and make you pay attention to issues you may not have otherwise recognized. So, why not use one of the critical theories profiled in this book to consider a fresh take on your favorite movie?

First, choose a theory and the movie you want to analyze. Remember that the theory is a springboard for asking questions about the work.

Next, write a specific question that relates to the theory you have selected. Then you can form your thesis, which should provide the answer to that question. Your thesis is the most important part of your critique and offers an argument about the work based on the tenets, or beliefs, of the theory you are applying. Recall that the thesis statement typically appears at the very end of the introductory paragraph of your essay. It is usually only one sentence long.

After you have written your thesis, find evidence to back it up. Good places to start are in the work itself or journals or articles that discuss what other people have said about it. Since you are critiquing a movie, you may also want to read about the director's life to get a sense of what factors may have affected the creative process. This can be useful if working within historical or auteur types of criticism.

Depending on which theory you apply you can often find evidence in the movie's language, plot, or character development. You should also explore parts of the movie that seem to disprove your thesis and create an argument against them. As you do this, you might want to address what other critics have written about the movie. Their quotes may help support your claim.

Before you start analyzing a work, think about the different arguments made in this book. Reflect on how evidence supporting the thesis was presented. Did you find that some of the techniques used to back up the arguments were more convincing than others? Try these methods as you prove your thesis in your own critique.

When you are finished writing your critique, read it over carefully. Is your thesis statement understandable? Do the supporting arguments flow logically, with the topic of each paragraph clearly stated? Can you add any information that would present your readers with a stronger argument in favor of your thesis? Were you able to use quotes from the movie, as well as from other critics, to enhance your ideas?

Did you see the work in a new light?

Timeline

1958 Tim Burton is born in Burbank, California, on August 25.

1979 Burton takes a job at Disney as an animator.

1999 *Sleepy Hollow* comes out to critical acclaim.

2010 *Alice in Wonderland* is another addition to Burton's list of remakes.

2003 *Big Fish* gains much critical success.

2005 *Corpse Bride* is another successful stop-motion animation feature film.

2007 *Sweeney Todd* is Burton's first remake of a musical.

1982 Burton produces *Vincent*, a stop-motion animation short.

1984 Burton creates *Frankenweenie*.

1985 Burton makes his first feature film, *Pee-wee's Big Adventure*.

1988 *Beetlejuice* establishes Burton's unique style in a feature film.

1989 *Batman* achieves record-breaking box-office success.

1990 *Edward Scissorhands* receives critical acclaim.

1992 *Batman Returns* comes out to mixed reviews.

1993 *Tim Burton's The Nightmare Before Christmas* is Burton's first stop-motion animation feature.

1994 *Ed Wood* is Burton's first commercial failure.

Glossary

aesthetic
> Dealing with beauty, art, and taste.

backlit
> When the source of illumination is behind the subject.

capitalistic
> A way of organizing an economy so that the things that are used to make and transport products are owned by individual people and companies rather than by the government.

compendium
> A collection of things (such as photographs, stories, and facts) that have been gathered together and presented as a group, especially in the form of a book.

consensus
> A general agreement about something.

covet
> To very much want something that you do not have.

deface
> To ruin the surface of something.

exotic
> Very different, strange, or unusual.

indefatigable
> Able to work or continue for a very long time without becoming tired.

juxtapose
>   To place different things together in order to create
>   an interesting effect or to show how they are the
>   same or different.

mantra
>   A word or phrase that is repeated often or that
>   expresses someone's basic beliefs.

ostracize
>   To not allow someone to be included in a group.

stop-motion
>   A filming technique in which objects (such as clay
>   models) are photographed in a series of slightly
>   different positions so that the objects seem to move.

Bibliography of Works and Criticism

Important Works

Pee-wee's Big Adventure, 1985

Beetlejuice, 1988

Batman, 1989

Edward Scissorhands, 1990

Batman Returns, 1992

Tim Burton's The Nightmare Before Christmas, 1993

Ed Wood, 1994

Batman Forever, 1995

Mars Attacks!, 1996

Sleepy Hollow, 1999

Planet of the Apes, 2001

Big Fish, 2003

Corpse Bride, 2005

Charlie and the Chocolate Factory, 2005

Sweeney Todd, 2007

Alice in Wonderland, 2010

Critical Discussions

Bassil-Morozow, Helena. *Tim Burton: The Monster and the Crowd: A Post-Jungian Perspective*. New York: Routledge, 2010. Print.

Gallo, Leah. *The Art of Tim Burton*. Los Angeles: Steeles, 2009. Print.

McMahan, Alison. *The Films of Tim Burton: Animating Live Action in Contemporary Hollywood*. New York: Continuum, 2005. Print.

Wisniewska, Dorota J. "Strangers in the Strange Land: The Gothic Mode in Tim Burton's Films." *American Studies*. 20: 2003 (143-156). Print.

Resources

Selected Bibliography

Bassil-Morozow, Helena. *Tim Burton: The Monster and The Crowd: A Post-Jungian Perspective*. London: Routledge, 2010. Print.

Fraga, Kristian. *Tim Burton: Interviews*. Jackson: UP of Mississippi, 2005. Print.

Hanke, Ken. *Tim Burton: An Unauthorized Biography of the Filmmaker*. Los Angeles: Renaissance, 1999. Print.

Further Readings

Giannetti, Louis D. *Understanding Movies*. Boston: Allyn & Bacon, 2011. Print.

Lynette, Rachel. *Tim Burton: Filmmaker*. San Diego: KidHaven, 2006. Print.

Thompson, Frank. *Tim Burton's Nightmare Before Christmas: the Film, the Art, the Vision*. New York: Hyperion, 2009. Print.

Web Links

To learn more about critiquing the films of Tim Burton,
visit ABDO Publishing Company online at
www.abdopublishing.com. Web sites about the films of
Tim Burton are featured on our Book Links page. These
links are routinely monitored and updated to provide the
most current information available.

For More Information

American Film Institute

2021 N. Western Avenue, Los Angeles, CA 90027

323-856-7600

www.afi.com

AFI is a nonprofit organization devoted to educating the
public about film and to promoting excellence in many
areas of filmmaking.

International Animated Film Society

ASIFA Hollywood, 2114 W Burbank Boulevard,
Burbank, CA 91506

818-842-8330

www.asifa-hollywood.org

This nonprofit organization supports the art of animation
through education and promotion.

Source Notes

Chapter 1. Introduction to Critiques
None.

Chapter 2. A Closer Look at Tim Burton
None.

Chapter 3. An Overview of *Batman*
1. *Batman*. Dir. Tim Burton. Warner Brothers, 1989. Film.
2. Ibid.
3. Ibid.
4. Ibid.
5. Ibid.
6. Ibid.

Chapter 4. How to Apply Cultural Criticism to *Batman*
1. *Batman*. Dir. Tim Burton. Warner Brothers, 1989. Film.
2. Ibid.
3. Ibid.
4. Ibid.

Chapter 5. An Overview of *Edward Scissorhands*

1. *Edward Scissorhands*. Dir. Tim Burton. Twentieth Century Fox, 1990. Film.

2. Ibid.

3. Ibid.

4. Ibid.

5. Ibid.

6. Ibid.

7. Ibid.

Chapter 6. How to Apply Biographical Criticism to *Edward Scissorhands*

1. Mark Salisbury. *Burton on Burton*. London: Faber and Faber, 1995. Print. 1.

2. Ibid.

3. Paul A. Woods. *Tim Burton: A Child's Garden of Nightmares*. London: Plexus, 2002. Print. 5.

4. Ibid.

5. *Edward Scissorhands*. Dir. Tim Burton. Twentieth Century Fox, 1990. Film.

6. Ibid.

7. Ibid.

Chapter 7. An Overview of *Sweeney Todd*

1. *Sweeney Todd: The Demon Barber of Fleet Street*. Dir. Tim Burton. Dream Works/Warner Brothers, 2007. Film.

Chapter 8. How to Apply Marxist Criticism to *Sweeney Todd*

1. *Sweeney Todd: The Demon Barber of Fleet Street*. Dir. Tim Burton. Dream Works/Warner Brothers, 2007. Film.

2. Ibid.

3. Ibid.

4. Ibid.

5. Ibid.

Chapter 9. An Overview of *Alice in Wonderland*

1. *Alice in Wonderland*. Dir. Tim Burton. Disney, 2010. Film.

2. Ibid.

3. Ibid.

4. Ibid.

5. Ibid.

6. Ibid.

7. Ibid.

8. Ibid.

9. Ibid.

Chapter 10. How to Apply Feminist Criticism to
Alice in Wonderland

1. *Alice in Wonderland*. Dir. Tim Burton. Disney,
2010. Film.

2. Ibid.

3. Ibid.

4. Ibid.

5. Ibid.

6. Ibid.

7. Ibid.

8. Ibid.

9. Ibid.

Index

About the Author

Sun Hee Teresa Lee teaches and writes about American literature and film at Gustavus Adolphus College in Minnesota. In her profession, she values critical thinking, meaningful exchange of ideas, and intellectual and ethical development.

Photo Credits

Anthony Harvey/PictureGroup via AP IMAGES, cover, 3; Jag Gundu/Stringer/Getty Images, 12, 98; Koichi Kamoshida/Getty Images, 17, 99; Warner Bros./Photofest, 18, 25, 26, 30; Zade Rosenthal/Twentieth Century Fox/Photofest, 38, 52; Fox/Photofest, 46; Leah Gallo/DreamWorks LLC and Warner Bros. Entertainment/Photofest, 58, 62, 64; Peter Mountain/DreamWorks LLC and Warner Bros. Entertainment/Photofest, 66; Walt Disney Pictures/Photofest, 76, 79, 82, 84, 91